CHAPTER I

A short but extraordinary life

I'm not sure whether you've realized but Jesus is one of the biggest things on our planet. He really is. People have estimated there are about two billion Christians on the planet today. They probably aren't all devoted Bible-believing legit followers of Christ— lots probably tick the 'Christian' box on a government form just because it's the closest thing they identify with, religiously speaking. If there were an option to tick 'Jedi knight', we might find the number of 'Christians' dropped markedly. But still, this Christianity thing has grown crazy big.

When you consider that Christianity is such an important feature of the world today, you might be surprised at the humble beginnings of its founder, Jesus Christ. According to the four gospels—Matthew, Mark, Luke and John, which are like biographies of the life of Jesus—about 2,000 years ago angelic messengers visited a young, engaged woman called Mary. After she recovered from the initial shock, they told her that she would give birth to a baby boy who would be none other than the Son of God, the one for whom God's people had been waiting for centuries. This child was not conceived in the usual human manner, but was conceived inside Mary's womb in the power of the Holy Spirit. However, the child did arrive in the usual human manner; nine months passed and the time came for the baby to be born, just as Mary and her fiancé Joseph went to register at a government census.

If you've ever celebrated Christmas, you probably know the story: all the hotels had *No Vacancy* signs out, and so this young unmarried woman gave birth to Jesus in a stable. Although the Christmas carols paint a pretty rosy picture of this birthing environment, I could not imagine a less inviting place to squeeze new human life out into the world. I'm guessing the cattle weren't lowing or singing a cow lullaby, because I've never seen a cow do that. They were more likely chewing, mooing and pooing, which after all is what cows do. And the other animals were probably not much better behaved. But in those crude and primitive surroundings, Jesus Christ the Son of God was born.

As was the custom for Jewish baby boys, Jesus was presented at the temple in Jerusalem before the Lord God, and then his parents went back to their hometown—a backwater place called Nazareth in Galilee. (If you're in America or Europe, think of Australia. If you're in Australia, think of Tasmania. If you're in Tasmania, think of New Zealand. If you're in New Zealand, I'm praying for you. No, really I am.) When he was twelve, at the end of a visit to Jerusalem, his parents accidentally left him behind. It took them three days to find him. That sounds a little like they were having a bender in Las Vegas, but it's more likely that they thought he was with relatives or friends also in their travelling group, because just about everyone had gone to Jerusalem that week for a national holiday. Jesus certainly wasn't running amok either; he was having deep and meaningful conversations with the religious leaders right there in the Jerusalem temple.

Other than that, we know very few other details about his early life.

In the gospels, we learn that "Jesus grew in wisdom and stature, and in favour with God and men" (Luke 2:52). But we hear very little about the next part of his life until he bursts forth into the wilderness of the Jordan Valley, where John the Baptist was baptizing people (that is, dunking them into the river to symbolize that they had turned away from their sins and back to God). In order to identify with us and show us that he was truly human even though he had never sinned, Jesus was baptized by John the Baptist along with the crowds. And then to show us that though he was truly human, he was the most remarkable human, he entered the wilderness for testing for a period of 40 days, during which time he was repeatedly tempted by Satan but never buckled under the pressure.

He was about 30 years old by this stage. Having commenced his public ministry, he devoted himself to a semi-nomadic life, travelling around preaching and teaching about the kingdom of God and his own central place within it. He gathered a core group of 12 fairly ordinary fellows around him, who became known as the disciples or sometimes just "the Twelve". And as he performed miracles, healings and exorcisms along the way, large crowds also began to follow him. He was known for his authoritative teaching, his empathy and friendship with outsiders, his love of children, and a certain laxity with some of the more rigid Jewish traditions that had developed by that time.

He increasingly became at odds with the Jewish religious leaders, such as the teachers of the Old Testament law and the scribes and many Pharisees. Not only was he relaxed about the Jewish traditions to which they were so attached, but as Jesus continued to garner a following, the Jewish religious figures felt he was a growing threat to their control over the Jewish people and religion. Though this tension was apparent at many times within the last three years of Jesus' life, it boiled over when he was in Jerusalem once again. The Jewish religious leaders and the Roman political leaders conspired to arrest Jesus on fabricated charges; they tried him before an unjust and unlawful court; and they sentenced him to death by crucifixion, the most horrible and humiliating of deaths then known to man.

Jesus lived a short but extraordinary life.

However, many people live short and extraordinary lives. The question is, why has this one life changed history more than any other? How can Jesus' 33 years on earth, over 20 centuries ago, result in a movement like Christianity that remains one of the biggest influences on our world to this day?

Jesus never went to high school or university. He never wrote a book or went into politics. He didn't marry, he didn't have children and he didn't own a home. He did not backpack around Europe or venture more than 200 km from his hometown.

He did few of the things that other 'great' people have done. When crowds wanted more from him, he withdrew from them. He had no credentials but himself. When he was given over to his enemies and sentenced to death on a cross, his executioners gambled for the only piece of property he had on earth—the simple woven shirt he had worn. After he died, his body was laid in a borrowed grave provided by a sympathetic friend.

Twenty centuries have come and gone, and today the Lord Jesus Christ remains a central figure of the human race. His birth divides our history into two eras—BC (Before Christ) and AD (Anno Domini, the Year of our Lord). The first day of every week is set aside in remembrance of him. And our two most important holidays—Christmas and Easter—celebrate his birth and death. The symbol of his death, the cross, can be seen on church towers all around the world. His life has been the subject of more songs, books and paintings than any other person or event in history. Thousands of colleges, hospitals, orphanages and other institutions have been founded in honour of him. It is no exaggeration to say that no army that ever marched, no navy that ever sailed, no government that ever sat, and no king that ever reigned has left as much of a lasting impression on the course of history as this one solitary life.

To understand why this is the case, we need to look more closely at the life and work of Jesus Christ. So we are going to think about three basic questions concerning Jesus: who he was (and is), what he came to do, and what he wants for us and from us.

Let's get rolling.

CHAPTER 2

Who is Jesus?

I suppose there are hundreds of different ideas about Jesus, about who he was and who he is today. As we saw in the first chapter, Jesus' influence has spread far and wide, particularly when you think about how localized his life was for his short time on earth. But just because this man has had an impact on almost every culture and almost every generation doesn't mean that everyone has a generally accurate idea about him. There are hundreds of different ideas as to who this man really was and is.

For example, I have seen plenty of 'pictures' of Jesus. Of course, there's the classic picture of Jesus with long, smooth hair, like he just stepped out of a hairdressing salon. In these depictions he usually has pale blue eyes and either rosy red cheeks or pale white skin as if a vampire had attacked him. There's often some sort of glow behind his head that looks like it's contributing to global warming. And if there's no glow, the artist sometimes draws a halo around Jesus' head. It can look more like a frisbee if you don't know what you're looking for.

But this classic European Jesus is not the only picture of Jesus floating about. It's not only white Europeans who create Jesus in their own image—I've seen pictures of a black African Jesus and an Asian Jesus. I've even seen a picture of a Mexican Jesus, complete with a sombrero instead of a halo, a twin gauge pump-action shotgun and a bandolier full of bullet casings. I've seen pictures of Jesus with little children, with little lambs, and with golf clubs, acting as a caddy for a famous golfer. People think they've seen him appear in cloud formations, in satellite pictures and even on a piece of burnt toast.

Jesus according to his closest followers

So there's no shortage of different ideas about Jesus. But if you want to get an informed opinion about Jesus, you need to consult someone other than old-school painters or cheeky Photoshop whizzes. You need to go back in time and space to get as close to the historical person of Jesus as you can. And as I mentioned in the first chapter, we have four separate historical accounts of Jesus in the four Gospels that open our New Testaments. There is a short section in one of those Gospels, Mark 8, which is worth camping out in for this part of the book.

Just to set the scene, the first half of Mark investigates the very question we are considering in this chapter: *Who is Jesus?* The people we meet in the first half of Mark openly ask this question in different ways at different times. But it all comes to a head when Jesus himself poses the question to his closest friends and followers. We might as well go straight to the text in this turning point of Mark's Gospel:

> Jesus and his disciples went on to the villages around Caesarea
> Philippi. On the way he asked them, "Who do people say I am?"
>
> They replied, "Some say John the Baptist; others say Elijah; and
> still others, one of the prophets."
>
> "But what about you?" he asked. "Who do you say I am?"
>
> Peter answered, "You are the Christ."
>
> Jesus warned them not to tell anyone about him. (Mark 8:27-30)

We'll return to this conversation between Jesus and Peter and the other disciples in the following chapters. But for now it is interesting to see a couple of things.

Firstly, we see that even back then there were plenty of different ideas about Jesus in circulation. Some thought he was John the Baptist (which is a little weird because John the Baptist had been executed by Herod a few chapters earlier—see Mark 6:14-29). Others thought he was Elijah, who was perhaps the most famous of Old Testament prophets (see 1 Kings 17-19); Elijah was taken up to heaven without dying (see 2 Kings 2:1-16), and the Jews expected him to make a comeback at some point (see Malachi 4:5-6). Still other people didn't seem to rate Jesus highly enough to be Elijah, and just settled on him being a prophet more generally.

Secondly, and way more importantly, we see Jesus' own view of who he was, which Peter the disciple lands on when he says to Jesus, "You are the Christ". That Jesus sees himself as "the Christ" is clear because instead of telling Peter that he's as dense as a lamb chop (which Jesus is more than willing to do when it's called for), Jesus warns all the disciples to keep this news to themselves, at least at this stage. The time for the message to go public would arrive soon enough.

So we understand that both Peter and Jesus think Jesus is "the Christ". The next obvious question is: *Who or what is the Christ?*

For starters, 'Christ' is not Jesus' surname as though it could just as easily have been 'Kelly' or 'Richards' or 'Johnson'. "The Christ" is a title. In Greek, which is the language the New Testament was written in, the word Christ literally means "the anointed one" (the same word in the Old Testament language of Hebrew is *Messiah*). Anointing was the sign of (a) being chosen by God, to (b) serve him in a particular way (and be equipped for that task). In the Old Testament, kings like David and Solomon were anointed, priests like Aaron were anointed, and the leaders of foreign nations were spoken of as having been anointed by God. Even the furniture was anointed in religious structures like the tabernacle and the temple. All these people and things were chosen by God to serve him in a particular way.

And yet the Israelites, God's people of old, looked forward to the coming of *the* Christ. They knew the Christ to be God himself: a God-appointed saviour, and a God-approved lord over everything. The Christ would be divinely chosen—anointed by a prophet, and publicly affirmed and empowered for leadership by the Holy Spirit. This is all tied up in what Peter meant when he called Jesus "the Christ", and when Jesus accepted that description of himself.

Of course, you might think that the stuff written about Jesus in the gospels of Matthew, Mark, Luke and John is just made up by men; perhaps it is just their spin on the life of Jesus. But it is worth remembering that we have more hard information about the existence of Christ than we do about most other historical figures of his time. This information is contained not only in the four separate eyewitness accounts of Jesus' life in the gospels, but also in historical sources outside the Bible.

It's also important to realize that the gospels are generally more descriptive than interpretive—that is, they record what happened more than they give their own interpretation or spin on the recorded events.

We also need to remember that many of the disciples and early Christians were executed for their testimony to Jesus, and all of them suffered persecution. You'd think that if you just made stuff up about Jesus, you'd be pretty keen to let your executioners know—at some stage before they cut your head off or tried to boil you to death—that you were only having a laugh.

The evidence

So if I'm going to make claims about the evidence that points to Jesus being the Christ, you probably want to see some of it, right? To put it another way, we want to work out from the available evidence whether Peter got it right when he confessed that Jesus is the Christ.

Outside evidence

Firstly, there is plenty of historical data from outside the text of the New Testament. On this front, we have references from over 100 non-Christian sources (e.g. Jewish and Roman historians). To give you a little of the flavour of some of these external historical sources, have a read of this snippet from a fellow called Publius Cornelius Tacitus. He was perhaps the greatest Roman historian of the era, and in AD 114 he wrote this in his *Annals of Imperial Rome* (make sure you spell that right!):

> Christians derive their name from a man called Christ, who during the reign of Emperor Tiberius had been executed by the sentence of the procurator Pontius Pilate. The deadly superstition, thus checked for the moment, broke out afresh not only in Judea, the first source of the evil, but also in the City of Rome, where all things hideous and shameful from every part of the world meet and become popular.[1]

It's pretty clear that Tacitus didn't like Christians or Christianity. He described Christianity as a "deadly superstition" and "hideous and shameful". And yet he made note of the person of Jesus Christ and his execution by Pontius Pilate, just as our gospels record. And he tells us that Christianity spread from Judea (where Jerusalem is) all the way to Rome, just as our New Testament tells us.

But is he the only one? You guessed it, the answer is no. In AD 110, Gaius Plinius Secundus (aka Pliny the Younger) was a Roman magistrate in northern Turkey. He wrote to Emperor Trajan, asking whether he should keep executing the Christians. This is what he said of them:

> The sum total of their guilt or error was no more than the following. They had met regularly before dawn on a determined day and sung a hymn to Christ as God.[2]

This shows that Pliny had been pretty nasty in the first place, killing Christians just because they sang *Amazing Grace* before breakfast. But it also confirms what we read in the New Testament—that the early Christians worshipped Jesus as God.

I'll give you one more. It's from a Jewish dude called Flavius Josephus who was employed by the Roman Emperor as an historian. He compiled a 20-volume work called *The Antiquities of the Jews*, which tells you everything you ever wanted to know about the history of Jewish people. Here's what this non-Christian historian said about Jesus:

> At this time lived a wise man named Jesus. He conducted himself well and was esteemed for his virtue. As many Jews as people from other nations became his disciples. Pilate condemned him to be crucified and put to death. But those who were his disciples did not cease to follow his teaching. They maintained that he appeared to them three days after his crucifixion and that he was alive.[3]

That sounds a lot like what we find in our New Testament, even though it was written independently.

All I'm saying is that you have a Roman historian and a Jewish historian who didn't like Christians, and a Roman magistrate who was killing Christians for singing before breakfast, all testifying to the same things as our New Testament. In fact, there are some 150 references to Jesus and the early Christians from 39 different sources outside the Bible. The Jesus we read about in Mark's Gospel and throughout the New Testament was no fictional figure.

As well as the many documents and fragments from back then that support the person and work of Jesus the Christ, there were plenty of homies too. In fact, by the AD 50s, just a few years after the death of Jesus, there were groups of people all around the eastern Mediterranean region who were convinced that a Jew named Jesus who had been executed in the early 30s was alive again and was "the Lord". One such group was the Corinthian Christians, who received a letter from the apostle Paul (a special spokesman of Jesus) that made extraordinary claims. This is what Paul wrote to the Corinthians:

> For what I received I passed on to you as of first importance: that Christ died for our sins according to the Scriptures, that he was buried, that he was raised on the third day according to the Scriptures, and that he appeared to Cephas (Peter), and then to the Twelve. After that, he appeared to more than five hundred of the brothers and sisters at the same time, most of whom are still living, though some have fallen asleep. Then he appeared to James, then to all the apostles, and last of all he appeared to me also…
> (1 Corinthians 15:3-8)

Now this is quite extraordinary because this letter was written probably in about 54 or 55 AD, well within the lifetime of people who were around when Jesus lived, died and rose again. It was a public document to be read aloud in church. This means that if its claims were ridiculous then the very people who observed the events of Jesus' life, death and resurrection would have challenged those claims. We could say a lot more about this little gem of a passage, but for now you just need to see that in a very short space of time there were groups of Christians gathering to worship and learn about Jesus.

So far, we have two sources of evidence testifying that Jesus is the Christ: the non-Christian historical record, and the early presence of churches all over the Mediterranean part of the world (from Spain all the way around the Middle East and then back into North Africa).

Inside evidence

I hope you're loving the outside evidence, but the inside evidence is way better. If we can put aside the rest of the New Testament for a moment (only because we don't have the space here to consider it all), let's consider the four records of the life of Jesus that were written within the lifetime of eyewitnesses:

- The Gospel of Mark was most likely a record compiled with Peter, although actually scribbled down by Mark.
- Matthew was written by one of Jesus' disciples (see Matthew 9:9).

- Luke says his gospel is a carefully researched account of eyewitnesses (see Luke 1:1-4).
- Finally, John was written by a disciple of Jesus (see John 21:24).

So what do the gospels say about Jesus? Can we reasonably conclude that he is the Christ, just as Peter confessed? To answer that question we need to investigate what the gospels say about the teaching of Jesus, the actions of Jesus, the death of Jesus, and his resurrection.

The teaching of Jesus

As we've already dipped into Mark's Gospel at chapter 8, we might as well stick with Mark's Gospel and begin at the beginning (if that's not too obvious).

Mark's Gospel is a little bit like a news update on TV. You're as happy as Larry, tuning into your favourite show on the box, when your viewing is rudely interrupted by a newsflash. The interruption comes because the news is urgent and important. You might get all the information later in the full news bulletin, but in a newsflash you'll only get the most important details. Mark's Gospel is like that. It is to the point. It has an urgency to it. It's the shortest of the gospels because it only tells you the most important details rather than including all the background information. And so unlike the gospels of Matthew and Luke, which include details about the birth of Jesus, Mark's Gospel begins by hastily introducing Jesus to us as a grown man about to begin his public ministry.

After being baptized and tempted in the desert, Jesus begins his public ministry by preaching and teaching. And the first impressions of his teaching are striking. Twice in the first chapter of Mark (verses 22 and 27), we see that people are amazed at his teaching because it has authority. His words are not like the words of other teachers and preachers; Jesus speaks with authority. Even demons obey him, and disciples too.

In some of his earliest recorded words, Jesus tells Simon Peter and his brother Andrew, two big burly fishermen, to follow him. He gives the same instruction to another set of brothers, James and John, who were nicknamed 'the Sons of Thunder' because they were pretty hot-tempered. Both sets of brothers leave their fishing nets and boats "at once" and "without delay" to follow Jesus. His teaching amazes people because he speaks with authority.

But what's interesting is that the main focus and central person in his preaching is none other than himself. He speaks broadly about the kingdom of God (1:15, 4:11, 4:26, 4:30) but instead of asking people to follow God, he asks people to follow himself. We can see this not only in his command to the rough-as-guts fishermen, but also in his commands to others throughout Mark's Gospel in different places and in different ways.

If you'd prefer to drop in on John's Gospel, the picture is equally clear. In John's biography, Jesus makes a series of statements about himself that have been called the 'I am statements', because each of them start with the words *I am*. In John 6:35, Jesus says, "I am the bread of life"; in John 8:12, he says, "I am the light of the world"; in John 11:25, "I am the resurrection and the life"; and in John 14:6, "I am the way and the truth and the life".

Jesus is happy to talk about himself when he is speaking about the things of God and the kingdom of God. And he is equally happy to call people to himself and to follow him. If he was telling the truth in his teaching, then he is the Christ: God himself, a God-appointed saviour, and a God-approved lord over everything. If he wasn't telling the truth then he was a liar. There is really no in-between position you can take. If we take him at his word he is the Christ; if not, he's a shameless liar.

And if you think he was lying, then it's worth thinking about his actions.

The actions of Jesus

A few years ago, my family and I were fortunate enough to go to Disneyland in California. The Australian dollar was strong, we had saved very hard for a number of years, and I had so many holidays up my sleeve that my boss kept telling me I needed to start taking them. So we went to Disneyland. My youngest son was only three at the time but he was just tall enough to scrape into some of the more 'active' rides; you know, the ones that don't just involve sitting in a pretend *Winnie the Pooh* honeypot and trickling along train tracks at five miles per hour.

What I didn't realize is that being *tall* enough to get into the scarier rides doesn't mean you're *old* enough to go on them. As we waited in line for the *Big Thunder Mountain* rollercoaster, we kept checking with my son to make sure he was keen for the ride. Because he'd been judged tall enough, he thought he was ready—that is, until we were all strapped in. A split second before we hurtled into the darkness at warp speed, he looked at me with white-faced horror and screeched, "Get me off!" What could I do? We were strapped in and away. For the next 2 minutes and 13 seconds he was shrieking like a banshee for the train to stop, but to no avail. Apparently the *Big Thunder Mountain* train stops for nothing. Once it left the station, it really was gone.

The early chapters of Mark are just like that rollercoaster at Disneyland. The speed at which Mark testifies to the actions of Jesus could be described as hurtling. He is relentless and you've just got to stay with it. If you take even a brief flick through these chapters, you'll see what I mean. Jesus drives out a violent evil spirit from one man with just a stern word (1:25), and then immediately heals Simon Peter's mother-in-law from her fever (1:29-31). Within a matter of hours the whole town turns up to be healed of their sicknesses and rid of their demons (1:32-34). The first chapter of Mark finishes with people coming to Jesus in droves after he heals a man with leprosy.

Chapter 2 opens with Jesus showing his authority over human sin when he heals a paralyzed man. At first glance, this miracle just looks like a continuation of the healing miracles from chapter 1. But if you read Mark 2:1-12 carefully you quickly discover that Jesus performs the outward action of physical healing to prove he has the authority to perform the inward spiritual action of forgiving the man's sins. Don't overlook the irony in the words of the sceptical Pharisees in Mark 2:7 when they exclaim, "Who can forgive sins but God alone?"

As these early chapters proceed, both Jesus' powerful words and his miraculous actions continue. He proves his authority over nature by calming a storm that threatens to swamp the boat he is sharing with the disciples (4:35-41). By the end of chapter 5, he has reached into death itself to raise a girl back to life. In the stillness of the waters, as the cowering disciples recover from the storm they thought would kill them, they ask one another this question: "Who is this?"

What an excellent question to ask ourselves. If his actions show his authority over demons, disease, sin, nature and even over death, then Jesus is the Christ: God himself, a God-appointed saviour, and a God-approved lord over everything. That is the most straightforward conclusion to draw. His actions back up his words; his miracles support the claims he made in his teaching. The only other conclusion you can draw is that he was a legend, a mythical hero of epic proportions. He was Superman without the tights, Spiderman without the web shooter thingies, Gladiator without the Hollywood paycheck.

But if you think Jesus was just a legend, remember he had to die and then, extraordinarily, rise again from the dead.

The death and resurrection of Jesus

Have you ever felt like there was something you just *have* to do? Perhaps you have your own 'bucket list' of things you really want to do in your life, like bungee jumping or rafting down the Zambezi River. I've done some extensive research on bucket list ideas and have seen some fairly bizarre things that people feel like they have to do in order to have lived a full life—including milking a cow, getting a kitten and being a vegetarian for a year. It's good to aim high! A few years ago I realized that there were only two things on my list: reading Victor Hugo's classic (and epically long) novel *Les Miserables*, and seeing the Grand Canyon with my own eyes. I've done both of those things now, so you might think I'm ready to die. But in all honesty, I never really *had* to do either of those things; I could have lived a full and interesting life without either of them. And now that I have done both of them, I don't feel all that prepared to leave this life.

When it comes to the life of Jesus, the one thing he saw as an absolute necessity was his own death. No skydiving or visiting the Grand Canyon or sticking to veggies for a year. Just one verse on from the passage in Mark 8 we looked at earlier, Jesus tells Peter that he *must* be killed and then rise again. Dying was an absolute necessity for Jesus, and we'll look at what that achieved in the following chapter.

But Jesus' death does not follow the normal Hollywood script of a hero's death. In the garden of Gethsemane, Jesus battles and struggles to follow through in going to the cross on behalf of sinful humanity. That would look almost embarrassing on screen. And his death on a Roman cross is not only brutal but also deeply shameful; there was no means of death as humiliating and dishonourable. Jesus was no mythical legend or hero of epic proportions. His death was the absolute 'must do' of his life, yet it was anything but heroic in the typical sense of that word.

Jesus' death on the cross for our sins to bring us back to God, in fulfilment of his own predictions, shows that he was the Christ, the God-appointed saviour of the world.

Of course, lots of people die mistakenly thinking they are someone special. Lots of people die for causes, for better or worse. Perhaps Jesus was just another lunatic in a long line of lunatics, or at the very least sadly mistaken.

And if he remained dead, then he would indeed join a long list of people who had died for a cause and remained dead. You would be entitled to conclude that he was a lunatic who thought he was God, but whose death proved beyond doubt that he was just as mortal as the next man.

But on that Sunday morning when Jesus stepped out of the tomb and out of death itself, everything changed—because the resurrection of Jesus is the conclusive proof that Jesus is the Christ. It validates everything he said about himself, everything he claimed about the purpose of his life, and everything he did in his most remarkable short life.

"You are the Christ", said Peter. From the evidence available we can see that Peter got it right when he uttered these words to Jesus so many years ago. Jesus is God himself, a God-appointed saviour, and a God-approved lord over everything.

The reason for God

Well what does all this mean for us? For a start, it means we can know for sure that God exists.

People typically try to prove the existence of God by using a number of pretty well worn philosophical arguments. They might argue that the existence of a universe, a something rather than nothing, requires a supreme being to account for it. They might say the great evidence of design and purpose in the universe requires a universal designer; or, more pointedly, that the fundamental regularity of physics and the fine-tuning of nature that gives rise to our universe and planet are so mathematically unlikely to occur by accident, it proves that God exists. Perhaps they could argue that the belief in a supreme creator god amongst all cultures across almost all ages, or the existence of universal moral values, also proves the existence of a transcendent God. Or even perhaps that the way we live life as though there is meaning and purpose, and the fact that there are things such as love and beauty in existence, signify that we are more than just random accidents in a meaningless cosmos.

Well, all of these arguments have a place, particularly if they are treated as clues rather than proofs for the existence of God, as Tim Keller argues in his excellent book *The Reason for God*.[4] But if Jesus is the Christ, and if part of being the Christ is being God himself—as the Old Testament prophets, the New Testament writers, and Jesus himself claimed it was—then we have our reason for God. Jesus is the reason for God. If Jesus is God and if he appeared as a matter of historical fact, then we know God exists. Even more, we know what God is like because when we see Jesus, we see God. The writer of Hebrews reminds us of this:

> In the past God spoke to our forefathers through the prophets
> at many times and in various ways, but in these last days he has

spoken to us by his Son, whom he appointed heir of all things, and through whom also he made the universe. The Son is the radiance of God's glory and the exact representation of his being, sustaining all things by his powerful word. (Hebrews 1:1-3a)

God revealed himself to his people of old in many different ways at many different times, but Jesus is God's final, ultimate and fullest revelation of himself. Jesus is God's greatest message. He is the radiance of God's glory and the exact representation of his being. In other words, when you see Jesus, you see God. Jesus, the Christ, is *the* reason for God.

Still the Christ?

But despite knowing that God exists and knowing what God is like from seeing what Jesus is like, you might still be wondering what he really has to do with you in this day and age. Sure, he *was* the Christ for the people of his day. He healed people back then and calmed a storm over there. But what has that got to do with you right here and right now?

To answer that question, we need to look much more closely at what Jesus really came to do. And that is where we are heading next.

CHAPTER 3

What did Jesus come to do?

Each year, as part of my job, I ask different groups of 16-year-olds to write down the names of three people in history who are really famous, and to write down what they're famous for. I tell them not just to pick someone who is famous today, like the current President of the United States or members of the latest boy band, but also to include people whose fame spreads across time and across different cultures. As you can imagine, the results are fairly predictable. Gandhi, Nelson Mandela and Mother Theresa usually make an appearance on the list; Adolf Hitler, Joseph Stalin and Pol Pot also normally get a mention for more sinister reasons. One year, Leonardo DiCaprio appeared in the number two spot on too many lists to be coincidental, but he hasn't made the grade in the last few years. The point is that what these notable people achieved is pretty obvious (apart from Leo).

In the same exercise I ask the 16-year-olds what they think the average person in the street considers Jesus' greatest achievement to be. Again, the results are fairly predictable. Typically, they say that Jesus' claim to fame is one of the following: he was a great teacher; he was a really moral guy; he founded a new religion called Christianity; he was a miracle worker; he launched a movement against the religious institution of the day; he was just a good bloke.

But when we turn to Jesus' biographers—the fellows who wrote the four gospels—they have a different answer. Somewhat unexpectedly, they consider the great achievement of Jesus' life to be his death. If you look at the gospel accounts in Matthew, Mark, Luke and John, approximately half the words are devoted to the relatively short period of time leading up to Jesus' death and resurrection. You can readily see this in the striking twist in the conversation between Jesus, Peter and the other disciples in Mark 8. Let's drop in on that conversation just after the point where Peter said that Jesus is the Christ:

> He [Jesus] then began to teach them that the Son of Man must suffer many things and be rejected by the elders, chief priests and teachers of the law, and that he must be killed and after three days rise again. He spoke plainly about this, and Peter took him aside and began to rebuke him.

> But when Jesus turned and looked at his disciples, he rebuked Peter. "Get behind me, Satan!" he said. "You do not have in mind the things of God, but the things of men." (Mark 8:31-33)

According to Jesus, referring to himself here as "the Son of Man", he had to suffer many things including rejection and ultimately his own death. We saw briefly in the last chapter that death was the 'must do' thing in his life. It was an absolute necessity for him. It was what he came to do, and he spoke so plainly about it that Peter the disciple took exception to the idea. In Peter's mind, it was incomprehensible that the Christ would suffer, be rejected and die. That's because Peter was expecting the Christ to be a king in the political or military sense of the word, and he thought the Christ would deliver the Jewish people from the hands of the Roman Empire, who ruled and oppressed them at the time. Peter was thinking about the role of the Christ in a merely human way. We might even call it a satanic way, in the sense that such reasoning was the opposite of God's plans for the Christ. There would be no great political or military victory against the Romans. According to Jesus, he would suffer, be rejected, and then die. That is what he came to do.

That is such an extraordinary thing to say and to think about, that it is worth quoting Mark's account of Jesus' death at length:

"What shall I do, then, with the one you call the king of the Jews?" Pilate asked them.

"Crucify him!" they shouted.

"Why? What crime has he committed?" asked Pilate. But they shouted all the louder, "Crucify him!"

Wanting to satisfy the crowd, Pilate released Barabbas to them. He had Jesus flogged, and handed him over to be crucified.

The soldiers led Jesus away into the palace (that is, the Praetorium) and called together the whole company of soldiers. They put a purple robe on him, then twisted together a crown of thorns and set it on him. And they began to call out to him, "Hail, king of the Jews!" Again and again they struck him on the head with a staff and spit on him. Falling on their knees, they paid homage to him. And when they had mocked him, they took off the purple robe and put his own clothes back on him. Then they led him out to crucify him.

A certain man from Cyrene, Simon, the father of Alexander and Rufus, was passing by on his way in from the country, and they forced him to carry the cross. They brought Jesus to the place called Golgotha (which means "the place of the skull"). Then they offered him wine mixed with myrrh, but he did not take it. And they crucified him. Dividing up his clothes, they cast lots to see what each would get.

It was the third hour [nine in the morning] when they crucified him. The written notice of the charge against him read: THE KING OF THE JEWS.

They crucified two robbers with him, one on his right and one on his left. Those who passed by hurled insults at him, shaking their heads and saying, "So! You who are going to destroy the temple and build it in three days, come down from the cross and save yourself!" In the same way the chief priests and the teachers of the law mocked him among themselves. "He saved others," they said, "but he can't save himself! Let this Christ, this King of Israel, come down now from the cross, that we may see and believe." Those crucified with him also heaped insults on him.

At the sixth hour [noon], darkness came over the whole land until the ninth hour [three in the afternoon]. And at the ninth hour Jesus cried out in a loud voice, "*Eloi, Eloi, lama sabachthani?*" (which means, "My God, my God, why have you forsaken me?")

When some of those standing near heard this, they said, "Listen, he's calling Elijah."

One man ran, filled a sponge with wine vinegar, put it on a stick, and offered it to Jesus to drink. "Now leave him alone. Let's see if Elijah comes to take him down," he said.

With a loud cry, Jesus breathed his last. (Mark 15:12-37)

The death of Jesus on the cross is such an extraordinary event that we need to understand it as fully and clearly as possible.

The cross in high definition

I don't know if you've ever heard people describe the gospel like this: "Jesus died to forgive my sins so that I can go to heaven". I have heard that flat description of Christianity so often that I've started to find it pretty irritating.

Don't misunderstand me; it's not that the description is wrong. But it is a one-dimensional, simplistic and flat understanding of what Jesus did for us on the cross. It's a good way of expressing the heart of Christianity if you're an 8-year-old in Sunday school. But if you're older than eight then I reckon we can do better, go deeper, and understand the cross in richer ways than that. It's the difference between seeing what Jesus' death does for us in a 3D, high-definition kind of way, and seeing it on an old-school black and white set. This might involve some hard thinking and big words, but I guarantee it's worth kicking that brain into gear.

But just before we do that, there are two things that we must understand.

The first is that our sin is a serious matter before God. We so often think of sin as just a random collection of small things that we do wrong. "Nobody's perfect," we say to ourselves, "everyone makes mistakes, so sin can't be that much of a big deal". But sin is not so much about the small things we do wrong as it is about a foundational attitude of the heart in which we rebel against God's rightful rule over our lives. It's the way in which we pathetically but predictably demand that we live our lives as we see fit, and worship anything and everything other than God, instead of honouring God with our lives and giving thanks to him and worshipping him. We tell God, with our lives and our hearts if not our lips, to butt out. The bad things we think, say and do—those things that often spring to mind when we hear the word 'sin'—are just the outward expression of our deep, inward attitude of rebellion against God and his rule over our lives.

The second thing we must wrap our brains around is the fact that God is rightfully angry with us for our sin. God's word declares that the wages of sin is death (Romans 6:23). In other words, what we deserve, what we have earned, is the rightful payment for our sin. And that is spiritual death, which involves being punished by God and cut off from his goodness forever.

You might feel like the punishment doesn't fit the crime. But our sin is not just an offence to the people we might have hurt, lied to or stolen from. It is primarily an offence against God. And the extent to which we think God's punishment is too severe is the extent to which we don't understand either the seriousness of our sin or the supreme holiness and perfection of the God we have so offended. Our sin is serious and real, and God's anger is righteous and will result in us being punished by God and cut off from his goodness and blessing. We are in a desperate situation, and our only hope can be found in the death of Jesus.

So what did Jesus' death really achieve for us?

Substitution

The first way to think about what Jesus' death achieved for us is often called 'substitution'. Put simply, substitution is *salvation by swap*. I say 'salvation by swap' because Jesus' death on the cross has got 'swap' written all over it.

For starters, the reason Jesus climbed onto the cross is because of our sin; and sin, at its heart, involves us swapping or rejecting our relatively lowly position as God's creatures and taking on God's position as rulers of our own lives. The punishment for that rejection, that foundational rebellious attitude at the heart of sin, is the very death that Jesus died.

Do we deserve death because of our sin? Yes.

Did Jesus deserve death for his perfectly righteous life? No.

Did Jesus experience both the just punishment of God and being cut off from relationship with God when he died upon the cross? Yes, he did.

Will we who trust in Jesus' death experience the just punishment of God for our sins and be cut off from relationship with him? No, we won't.

In our sinful rebellion, we put ourselves where God ought to be. But in his great mercy, Jesus put himself where we ought to be when he died for us, in our place, on the cross. Jesus was loaded with the penalty that we deserve for our sin, and we are gifted with the right standing with God that Jesus deserves. In our hearts we 'swap' our place for God's place as rightful ruler of our lives, which means we deserve punishment. But on the cross, Jesus swapped places with us. He took the punishment we deserve for our sin, and we get the benefit of the righteous life he lived in perfect obedience to God.

About 700 years before the birth of Jesus, the prophet Isaiah said these words to prepare us for what Jesus would do when he died on the cross:

> But he was pierced for our transgressions, he was crushed for our iniquities; the punishment that brought us peace was upon him, and by his wounds we are healed. We all, like sheep, have gone astray, each of us has turned to his own way; and the LORD has laid on him the iniquity of us all. (Isaiah 53:5-6)

If you look closely at those verses, the concept of 'swap' is all over the place. If you were to drag a highlighter across every instance in which Jesus' suffering and death was for us, every instance when he subbed in for us, there would probably be no unmarked words. That's substitution: salvation by swap.[5]

Justification

The second thing Jesus' death achieved for us is our 'justification'.

'Justification' is a legal kind of word, so to understand justification you need to imagine a law court with a judge. If you've ever been in a courtroom, you'll know that they are scary places. I have been to court a few times: once as a witness, once to be a member of a jury, and once to support a friend of mine who had been charged with a serious crime. Each time I found it to be daunting. The judge sits at a really high bench with his gown and robes on; he won't even talk to you or acknowledge your presence unless you're wearing a suit. When I was supporting my friend, I was sitting at the very back of the courtroom. During the afternoon I got bored, so I was trying to bounce the sun coming in through the window off my watch. Before I knew it, I realized that I was shining it right into the judge's eyes. That's when I realized I was an idiot and I had to stop because the judge can put you away. His courtroom is a serious place.

In the courtroom of life, God is the judge and we are the ones charged and guilty because of our sin. Whether or not we *feel* guilt, we *are* all guilty because we have all rebelled against God. Amazingly, for those with faith in the death of Jesus, God the judge makes a legal decision in our favour. Instead of treating us as guilty, he will not only forgive us our sins but also treat us as perfectly righteous—as righteous as his own Son Jesus was in his earthly life. He is the judge, so he gets to make that legal declaration. And he's not stupid or blind; he knows that we are not right with him, that we are not naturally righteous, and that we will continue to stuff up afterwards. But he still makes a decision in our favour not only to pardon our sin but also to treat us as righteous, just as Jesus was.

If our sins were only pardoned or forgiven, we would only go from being negative to being neutral. But with justification, God goes a step further and declares us to be righteous—to be 'justified'. He decides to treat us as perfectly good and righteous, like Jesus was in his earthly life. So, in that single declaration from God, we go not only from negative to neutral but also from neutral to positive. It is as if he is not only saying "Go, you're free", but also "Come near, you're actually good"—not because we are naturally good people, but because Jesus is good, and because God the judge makes that decision to treat us as though we share Jesus' goodness and righteousness.

Redemption

The third thing Jesus' death achieved for us is our 'redemption'. We talk about redeeming things all the time. For example, we talk about redeeming credit or gift cards at the iTunes store. Or we might say that an awful film was redeemed only by the extraordinary performance of one actor in the film, or something like that. When we use the word 'redemption' that way, we are usually saying that something good has compensated for something bad. But the biblical concept of redemption is even more specific and technical, so it helps to understand some of the background to this idea.

The biblical idea or picture of redemption is drawn from the slave market, which was a common feature in New Testament times. Slaves in New Testament times were not the same as the African slaves in the deep south of the United States that we often think about when we hear the word 'slave'. Slaves in New Testament days were not kidnapped; people voluntarily gave themselves as slaves to their masters, sometimes to pay off debts or even to advance in society. Slavery was not for an indefinite period, and slaves had rights that could be enforced in the courts. Slaves would occupy important positions in some households.

But they were not free. To gain freedom from their masters, someone else had to pay an amount of money on their behalf, called a ransom price. The payment of the ransom price redeemed the slave or set them free from their master. That's how redemption worked in New Testament times. (Actually, the Old Testament often talks about how God redeemed Israel from their slavery in

Egypt, so the concept goes back even further than New Testament times.)

The question is how this works in relation to Jesus' death for us. Mark 10:45, a well-known verse for good reason, puts it like this:

> For even the Son of Man did not come to be served, but to serve, and give his life as a ransom for many.

Jesus' death, the giving of his life, was the payment of a ransom for those who put their trust in him. This assumes that we are naturally slaves to sin, death and the devil. And it also assumes that we are unable to free ourselves, just as the slaves in New Testament times (or even God's people in slavery in Egypt) were unable to free themselves. The analogy does not extend to the details of to whom the ransom price is paid, but the Bible makes clear that Jesus' death is the ransom price that sets us free from our old slave masters of sin, death and the devil.

Propitiation

The next way the New Testament talks about what Jesus' death achieved is called 'propitiation'. Strange word, I know, and unlike the word 'redemption', we don't really use this word at all any more. Most of the Bibles we use these days translate the original word for propitiation as 'atonement' (e.g. Hebrews 2:17) or as 'a sacrifice of atonement' (e.g. Romans 3:25; 1 John 2:2, 4:10). So what does 'propitiation' actually mean?

Back in the Old Testament days of the Passover sacrifices—sacrifices that were offered in the temple in Jerusalem—people recognized that they were sinners. This meant they were the objects of God's wrath—that is, his righteous and appropriate anger at human sinfulness. But when the sinner brought a perfect or unblemished animal to be sacrificed, God would choose to pour his anger out on the animal instead of the person. And because God's anger was absorbed by the animal, it meant that his righteous anger was turned away from the person. God was no longer angry with that person, who could once again be in fellowship and relationship with God.

When the New Testament talks about Jesus' death as a propitiation for our sins (in places like Romans 3:25 and 1 John 2:2 and 4:10), it is telling us that we are rightly considered to be objects of God's anger. And it is telling us that when Jesus died as a *propitiation* for our sins, he absorbed all the righteous anger of God that we deserved, so that God is no longer angry with us. By absorbing all of God's anger upon himself in his death, Jesus has turned God's anger away from us. This really is wonderful news because it means that those of us who have faith in Jesus have no need to fear God's judgement. God is no longer angry with us. His anger has been turned away. God's punishment for our sin has been taken away, never to return again.

When you go fishing and you catch a fish that is a little too small to keep, you are supposed to take the hook out, give it a kiss on the lips and toss it back in the water. When you do that, the fish swims away, never to be seen again. That's no exaggeration—you will never see that fish again, ever. God's wrath—his anger and judgement at our sin and unrighteousness—is like that fish that swims away. When God presented Jesus as a propitiation, God's anger was turned away so that he is no longer angry with those who trust in Jesus. God's judgement will not fall upon those who trust in Jesus—not now, and not in the future. God is no longer angry with us because Jesus has absorbed all God's wrath that we deserved. It's never to be seen again. And if that doesn't make you burst out of your skin with joy, I don't think you properly understand the dangerous position we're naturally in because of our sin.

Reconciliation

The last thing Jesus' death achieved for us is what the New Testament calls 'reconciliation'. Reconciliation is the process by which two parties who were enemies are brought back into friendship and good standing with one another. Where some of the other ways of thinking about Jesus' death are drawn from quite specific parts of the culture and society in which the Bible was written, the idea of reconciliation is pretty straightforward. It's as if we've walked away from home—kind of like the prodigal son of Jesus' famous parable in Luke 15. We've walked out on God. We have become distant and estranged from him, even hostile enemies. But Jesus' death reconciles us back into relationship with God. Romans 5:10-11 says:

> For if, when we were God's enemies, we were reconciled to him through the death of his Son, how much more, having been reconciled, shall we be saved through his life! Not only is this so, but we also rejoice in God through our Lord Jesus Christ, through whom we have now received reconciliation.

We were God's enemies—whether that was passively (e.g. "I don't really care about God"), ignorantly (e.g. "I don't really know about God") or angrily (e.g. "I don't like God at all")—but now we have been reconciled to God through the death of Jesus. We were distant and estranged from God, but three times in these short verses we are told that we have now, through the death of Jesus, received reconciliation. Jesus' death has brought us home to God. Jesus' death has made peace between God and us. We are no longer his enemies but are now friends with God.

So there we have five ways of thinking about how the death of Jesus changes us and restores us back into right standing and friendship with God. Of course, there are plenty of other ways in which the Bible helps us to expand our understanding of everything Jesus did for us when he climbed on to that Roman cross outside the city of Jerusalem. But that's a decent start to thinking about the death of Jesus in high definition.

After the cross
When you watch a serious movie like a drama or suspense thriller, you know it's the end of the film when the screen goes dark, then there's an awkward pause when nothing happens, and then the credits start scrolling up the screen. That's a pretty standard way

to finish a film. But most of the animated films that come out of Hollywood these days not only have funny outtakes playing while the credits are rolling, they also have a final, pithy little scene at the end. It might involve singing and dancing lemurs or some little furry animal burping out the alphabet, or something like that. But it means that nowadays, the movie is not necessarily over when the screen goes dark; sometimes there's more to come.

As we've already seen in Mark 15, the sky certainly went dark when Jesus died even though it was the middle of day. But it wasn't over; there was more to come. We might be tempted to think, now that we have peered into what Jesus came to do by dying on the cross, that we are ready to think about what Jesus wants from us and for us. But just before we go there, we need to pause and remember that Jesus did not stay dead.

In a scene way more extraordinary than rodents belching out their ABCs, the Jesus story did not end in darkness. Another scene was yet to be played out. And in that scene, Jesus Christ rose again from the dead. On the third day, in accordance with the predictions of the Old Testament and of Jesus himself, and to the astonishment of the women who went to Jesus' tomb and the disciples who had chickened out and were in hiding, Jesus rose from the dead. Let's see how Mark records this extraordinary event:

> When the Sabbath was over, Mary Magdalene, Mary the mother of James, and Salome bought spices so that they might go to anoint Jesus' body. Very early on the first day of the week, just after sunrise, they were on their way to the tomb and they asked each other, "Who will roll the stone away from the entrance of the tomb?"
>
> But when they looked up, they saw that the stone, which was very large, had been rolled away. As they entered the tomb, they saw a young man dressed in a white robe sitting on the right side, and they were alarmed.
>
> "Don't be alarmed," he said. "You are looking for Jesus the Nazarene, who was crucified. He has risen! He is not here. See the place where they laid him. But go, tell his disciples and Peter, 'He is going ahead of you into Galilee. There you will see him, just as he told you.'"
>
> Trembling and bewildered, the women went out and fled from the tomb. They said nothing to anyone, because they were afraid. (Mark 16:1-8)

Jesus had truly died on that Friday afternoon, but on the third day—Easter Sunday—he walked out of the tomb alive. Jesus rose again; he was no longer dead in a tomb. All of the gospel accounts testify that Jesus rose again from death and is now alive, as does the remainder of the New Testament, from the first page of the book of Acts to the last page of Revelation. Hundreds saw him and heard him. Many ate with him. One famously put his fingers in the nail marks of the resurrected Jesus' hands, and into the spear wound in the resurrected Jesus' side, and then proclaimed that Jesus was both Lord and God.

The resurrection of Jesus is the event that forcefully confirms Jesus is the saviour, just as Peter had confessed way back in Mark 8. The resurrection of Jesus proves right everything that Jesus said. The resurrection is God's stamp of approval on everything that Jesus did. His death dealt with our sin, properly and effectively, once for all time. And his resurrection guarantees that we will follow him into eternal life. By virtue of Jesus' resurrection, Jesus is shown undeniably to be our long-awaited saviour.

The apostle Peter was transformed by the resurrected Jesus from a nervous witness who betrayed Jesus into a bold messenger of the good news. Peter testified that Jesus is not only the saviour, but that his resurrection means he is also Christ and Lord, the one who rules everything. In the first and extraordinary speech that

Peter gives following the ascension of Jesus back up to heaven, he says this to an audience of Jewish folk from around the world who had gathered in Jerusalem:

> God has raised this Jesus to life, and we are all witnesses of the fact… "Therefore, let all Israel be assured of this: God has made this Jesus, whom you crucified, both Lord and Messiah."
> (Acts 2:32, 36)

It was no accident that Peter was able to testify before people from all over the known world that Jesus is both Lord and Christ, because Jesus is the worldwide Lord and Christ. His resurrection means he is not only a local saviour for the nation of Israel, but also the worldwide Lord—the boss of everything, everyone, everywhere. This means that Jesus is now the one whom everyone should worship, and to whom everyone should bow down and confess, "You are the Christ".

Now if Jesus' death and resurrection achieves all these things, the obvious question is: How do I claim for myself all that Jesus has done for the world? *What does he want from me, and for me?* Turn the page, my friend—that's where we are headed next.

CHAPTER 4

What does Jesus want from me?

Every now and again, I find an offer in the mailbox from a car-servicing centre that is trying to win my business. I am always interested in what they offer—after all, I have to get my car serviced somewhere. They usually offer free petrol, which might sound a little dull, but when the price of petrol is as high as it is, they've got my attention. But, so far, I've never actually taken up their offer. The problem is not that what they're offering doesn't appeal to me—it does. The problem is that the steps to taking up the offer are just not straightforward at all.

It's fair enough that to get the free gas I have to take my car to their servicing centre, but it usually has to be at some ridiculously early (or late) timeslot, and I can only take it to the mechanic called Murray or Vinnie or something like that, and if I were to read the fine print I'd probably discover that I also have to dress up in a Stormtrooper costume on the day I take the car in. I'm interested in their offer but the process of claiming it is just not straightforward enough.

Is it the same with what Jesus offers? After discovering that Jesus was no mere man—he was God himself in the flesh—and learning about the good things that Jesus' death and resurrection achieved for us, we are naturally interested in how to claim those benefits personally. We're interested in the offer, but how do we access it? What does Jesus want from me, and more than that, what does he want *for* me?

In this chapter I want to explain as simply as possible that he wants lifelong relationship with him (eternal lifelong relationship, as it turns out) *for* us, and he wants wholehearted belief *from* us.

Eternal lifelong relationship

You probably don't know about Rollen Stewart, who is also known as Rockin' Rollen Stewart, who is also known as the Rainbow Man because he used to wear a rainbow-coloured afro wig. For years Rollen Stewart could be seen making a spectacle of himself at big sporting events across the United States. Through much practice and thousands of dollars, Rollen worked out where to strategically position himself in the grandstands—behind American football goalposts, near Olympic medal stands, next to the pits of NASCAR winners—to steal the limelight from the televised sporting events. He probably got a bit carried away, because the television networks hated him. The reason he was so careful about where he sat at events, and the reason the networks hated him, was that he would hold up a big sign during crucial moments of the sporting fixture so that his sign was broadcast across America. Millions of people saw his sign. ABC sports producer Chet Forte once said, "He would station himself behind home plate [in baseball] and our camera would view over the pitcher's shoulder and it was very annoying seeing this guy waving his sign".

In simple bold, black type, the sign read "John 3:16". Rollen claimed he was harassed at the 1980 Moscow Olympics by the secret police, who thought he was a spy and thought his John 3:16 sign was some sort of coded message. Of course, John 3:16 is not a coded spy message but is perhaps the most well-known verse in the Bible:

> "For God so loved the world, that he gave his one and only Son,
> that whoever believes in him shall not perish, but have eternal life."

One of the end goals of Jesus' life mission, of his death and resurrection, was to rescue us from destruction and to bring us eternal life. Jesus is about bringing life—eternal life—to people who put their trust in him.

When Christians think about eternal life, they often speak of it as though it were identical to and interchangeable with 'heaven'. So they usually have in mind a fine, white sandy beach, with crystal blue water gently lapping the shore, under a perfect cobalt sky and the shade of some coconut trees. Or they talk about eternal life and/or heaven as if it were a great theme park in the clouds, and Jesus' death bought us a ticket to this celestial tourist attraction. But I think they're wrong, because if either of those options were true then John 3:16 would read:

> "For God so loved the world, that he gave his one and only
> Son, that whoever believes in him shall not perish, but go to the
> Caribbean."

Or:

"For God so loved the world, that he gave his one and only Son, that whoever believes in him shall not perish, but get into Disneyland."

When Christians think of heaven or eternal life as being like a Caribbean beach or a holiday to Disneyland, they forget what the best part of heaven is. The best part of heaven is that we will be with Jesus. The last chapter of the Bible, Revelation 22, is a picture of what life will be like in the new heavens and new earth. And it hits its high point when it tells us in verse 4 that we will see Jesus' face. We will be with our heavenly Father and we will see the face of Jesus. Unbroken relationship with the Father and the Son is the reason heaven will be good, not white sand or the *Space Mountain* rollercoaster.

I'm not an especially touchy-feely, emotional kind of guy, but I reckon when I get to heaven I am going to run up to Jesus and hug him until it gets awkward. I don't think I'll let go until one of the angels taps me on the shoulder and tells me to move along because it's getting kind of embarrassing for everyone.

Even if heaven *were* a perfect Caribbean beach or an exhilarating Disneyland, without Jesus there it would quite simply be hell—

regardless of the number of coconuts. And if heaven were to turn out to be as squalid as the slums of Rio or Calcutta or the ghettos of Detroit, but with Jesus there, then that would be the best place for us to spend eternity. I'm confident it won't be like that, but the point is that the best thing God gives us is himself, not a beach. And the best part of eternity is not the holiday but the relationship with Jesus. So I cannot wait.

But here's the deal: I don't have to wait. Because heaven and eternal life are not identical and interchangeable. They are not exactly the same thing. And if eternal life is about relationship with the Father and Son more than anything else, then I already enjoy that now, don't I? That seems to be what Jesus says in John 17:3:

> "Now this is eternal life: that they may know you, the only true
> God, and Jesus Christ, whom you have sent."

Jesus came to live and die and rise again so that we might have eternal life rather than be forever destroyed. But in Jesus' own mind, eternal life is about relationship with him and with God the Father. So the goodness has already begun, and we have already started our eternal lives. Of course, we will know in full then what we only know in part now (1 Corinthians 13:12). What Jesus wants for us and from us is eternal lifelong relationship with him.

Our relationship with Jesus is not identical to a human relationship or friendship. We are not equals and we never will be. But we are loved. Loved in the sense that Jesus has our best interests at heart with everything he tells us to do—so obedience to him is neither arbitrary nor destructive to us. Loved in the sense that he's interested in the details of our lives, the ups and downs and the many decisions that make up every human day—so we can bring anything and everything before him in prayer. Loved in the sense that he will walk with us through this life and carry us into the next life—so we really can entrust our future and destiny to him. That's what the relationship is like. And we have only just begun to enjoy it.

Wholehearted belief

But to enter into that relationship and to obtain all the benefits of life with Jesus, the entry point appears to be belief. We've already seen in John 3:16 that those who believe in Jesus will not be destroyed but will have eternal life. This idea pops up time and again in John's Gospel—for example, just a few verses along in John 3:36:

> "Whoever believes in the Son has eternal life, but whoever rejects the Son will not see life, for God's wrath remains on him."

Belief clearly leads to eternal life. In other words, eternal life is accessed by genuine trust in Jesus' death in our place for our sins.

It is not available to those who instead want to trust in their own merit, moral performance or natural worthiness. Christians often talk about 'grace', which is the undeserved goodness of God towards undeserving people. The whole reason the news about Jesus is called the *good* news is because it shows undeserving, sinful people like us how we can be on good terms with God despite our hopeless moral performance and natural unworthiness. So this grace—the goodness of God in the death of his Son for us—is key, and belief is what leads to life. But what does Jesus really mean by 'belief'?

If we return to the Gospel of Mark, where we camped out in chapter 2, we hear Jesus say in Mark 8:34-35:

> "If anyone would come after me, he must deny himself and take up his cross and follow me. For whoever wants to save his life will lose it, but whoever loses his life for me and for the gospel will save it."

In both John's Gospel and Mark's Gospel Jesus talks about eternal life, and in both cases he talks about what is needed to get this eternal life. But it appears as if he contradicts himself. In John's Gospel Jesus says that belief leads to life, whereas in Mark's Gospel he talks about denying yourself, following him, and losing your life. It is not immediately obvious how these two different things can be reconciled.

Perhaps it might help to work out what Jesus *doesn't* mean when he makes these statements. For starters, when Jesus talks about losing your life for him, he is not saying he wants every Christian to be a martyr (that is, a Christian hero who is literally killed because of their faith in Christ). If that were the case then our eternal salvation would be on account of our own merits, our own goodness, our own work of martyrdom. But from all that we have seen so far, we know this cannot be the case.

But equally, when Jesus talks about belief, he is not saying that Christianity is a one-off intellectual decision that has no real bearing on the rest of our lives. Certainly, it *is* an intellectual decision. We choose to follow Jesus with our brains based on the facts available to us, in combination with faith. But it's more than a one-off decision. It's a decision that shapes the rest of our life.

The belief Jesus talks about in John's Gospel is *wholehearted belief*—not just *intellectual agreement* with the claims Jesus makes about who he is, what he did and what he wants from us. Wholehearted belief is the kind of muscular belief that Jesus talks about in those verses from Mark's Gospel. When Jesus says that life follows for those who "come after me", he is telling us that he wants to be *followed*, not just agreed with intellectually. The resurrected Lord of all things is commanding us to submit ourselves to him and to his rule. As the only one who has been pronounced Lord and Christ by God, following his rise from death, Jesus is asking us to turn from our old sinful ways of conducting our lives to following his desires and decrees for us. When he asks would-be followers to deny themselves, the kind of belief he is after is the kind of belief that pushes aside the selfish ambitions and desires we have for our own lives in favour of what he desires for our lives.

To some degree, when we choose Jesus we choose against ourselves. That's really what having a king, a lord, a boss, a Christ really means: we are not our own king, lord, boss or Christ. When Jesus talks about taking up our cross, he has a particularly vivid image in mind. These days, crosses have become fashion accessories, whether as jewellery, as tattoos or on clothing. But crosses in Jesus' day were instruments of torture and death. They were not trendy style items. Imagine wearing a necklace with a syringe filled with poison, or getting a tattoo of a guillotine or firing squad! When Jesus tells us to take up our cross, he wants us to put to death any right we think we have to run our life our way. He asks us to surrender all of our life to him. It's not that we can somehow earn our way into his favour and salvation through our devotion to him. But it is a wholehearted, all of life, muscular, gutsy kind of trust that Jesus has in mind. His idea of belief is much closer to our idea of full-bodied trust, loyalty and allegiance than it is to mere intellectual agreement.

Luke 14 is one of my all-time favourite chapters in the New Testament, for lots of reasons. One reason is that Jesus lays the smackdown on an important Pharisee, even while he's eating dinner at the Pharisee's house. I'm guessing he probably didn't get another invitation there. If you happen to think that Jesus is really into cuddling lambs and kittens like in some pictures, the start of Luke 14 is a good reminder that he's no pushover. Still at the dinner table, Jesus tells a story that has become known as the parable of the great banquet (in Luke 14:15-23). It's a terrific story where Jesus describes his kingdom as the party of the year.

The good news about this party is that, well, it's the party of the year—who doesn't love a good party? Even better is the news that entry is by invitation, which reminds us that you don't earn life with Jesus—you cannot work your way into his favour and you don't deserve his salvation. Entry is only by his amazingly gracious invitation, and everyone is invited.

But there's a sting in the tail of this story. The people who were first invited to the banquet make what can only be described as the most inane, ridiculous excuses for not accepting the invitation. One says he has just bought a field and is on his way to see it, as if the field will have somehow disappeared by morning. The next bloke says he's just bought some oxen, which are meaty work animals not smart enough even to be called cows. As if you'd miss out on the party of the year because of some dense farm animals! Another couple then say that they've been recently married so they cannot attend. For some reason, they think it will be more fun to stay at home watching *Top Gear* or *Man vs. Wild* than to attend the party of the year. It's a real sting in the tail because we don't want to miss out on life with Jesus because of dumb decisions and ridiculous excuses.

This biting parable makes us pay attention as Jesus paints three pictures in Luke 14:25-35 about what wholehearted belief looks like. The first picture is a family picture, in which he famously tells the crowds following him:

> "If anyone comes to me and does not hate his father and mother, his wife and children, his brothers and sisters—yes, even his own life—he cannot be my disciple." (verse 26)

Jesus sounds like he's being over-the-top by saying that his disciples must hate their families and even their own lives if they want to be with him. And in a way, he is—because in other parts of the gospels he reminds people to love and look after their parents. I take it that he's being deliberately provocative and extreme here so that we will realize that following Jesus is to take priority in our lives. Wholehearted belief makes Jesus number one, sometimes even at the expense of those nearest and dearest to us.

When I was a wee little fella, it was a real treat to go to the cinemas. Back in my day, there weren't cinemas in every suburban shopping centre like there is today. The only cinemas were in the city. And we only ever went in the school holidays. So my mum would bundle up my brother and sister and me, and we'd catch the train into town, meet my dad after work, and go to a movie. And

I remember that just outside the exit from Town Hall station, on one of the most prominent corners in the centre of the city, we'd see a big hole. By 'big', I mean that it took up about half a block of prime real estate in the middle of town. Someone had bought the block and dug down to lay some foundations, but then obviously ran out of money. So the big hole remained for years, to the shame of the poor bloke who ran out of cash before he finished—or even really started—his building.

In the second picture, in Luke 14:28-30, Jesus paints a similar picture of a person who wants to build a building. He suggests that if you don't want people to laugh at you, then before you dig your first hole you should work out if you have enough money to finish the project. The point of the story is to show us that belief in Jesus is not about making an off-the-cuff decision to follow him that hasn't been duly considered. Wholehearted belief in Jesus requires us to first count the cost of following Jesus. This means thinking through what it will mean to follow him, both positively and negatively, before jumping on board with Jesus.

The last picture is a picture of battle (14:31-33), in which Jesus says that a king will work out beforehand whether he can defeat an enemy that has more troops than he. Jesus is not saying that Christians will be outnumbered in this life; he is making the point that you really want to work out what it means to give up everything to follow him, before you climb on board the Jesus train.

It is possible, I suppose, that you could look at these pictures in Luke 14 and conclude that believing in Jesus is going to be too hard. Or that it's not worth the bother. If so, you need to remember that it is better to have life with Jesus than to gain the whole world. There is nothing worth exchanging your soul for, or your eternal life. Getting scared off from following Jesus would be a mistake. The pictures in Luke 14 aren't meant to *scare* us; they are meant to *prepare* us for the road ahead. Believing in Jesus wholeheartedly will involve cost, and Jesus is just being up front about that. He wants genuine belief from us, not just an intellectual acceptance of his gracious invitation. But he is holding out an offer of eternal lifelong relationship, and nothing is better than that.

Change you can believe in

Maybe you have read this book and are now asking yourself the question: *So what?* What difference does this all make in my life? Well, that depends whether you are a Christian or not. If you are a Christian, then I guess you need to take Jesus' words to heart: whoever wants to follow Jesus must deny himself, take up his cross, and follow Jesus. And I guess we need to settle in for the long haul, because the Christian life—the eternal life with Jesus that starts now—is more like a marathon than a sprint. However, life with Jesus is the best life there is, and it will only get better into eternity.

And remember that God will help you in the marathon of the Christian life. He will speak to you as you read his word, the Bible. He will listen to you and help you as you pray to him. He will strengthen you to live his way by his Spirit, who lives in all Christians. And he will provide brothers and sisters to help as you meet with other Christians in church.

If you are not yet a Christian, you might be wanting to find out more. So find out more. Read one of the gospels, or all of them. Talk to a Christian mate, or drag your good self along to a Bible-believing, Jesus-loving church. If you find the person and work of Jesus compelling, then don't leave it here. Take it further.

Perhaps you're at a point where you may not know everything about Jesus, but you know enough to want to take steps to become a wholehearted believer in Jesus. You may want to change—and this will be change you really can believe in. A first step, which millions of people have taken to become a follower of Jesus, is to pray honestly to God. Here's an example of what other people have said to God when they became Christians:

Dear God,

I know I do not deserve your love. I have ignored you, and rebelled against you. I'm sorry. I need your forgiveness and your salvation.

Thank you for sending your Son to die in my place. Thank you that he rose from the dead to give me new life.

Please forgive me and change me, that I might live with Jesus as my Lord and my God.

Amen.

If you have just prayed that prayer then I would personally like to welcome you into the Christian life, and into the community of Christ-followers around the world and over the centuries. You are definitely not alone.

As you start on this journey with Jesus as your Lord and God, there will be plenty of ups and down for sure, and not everyone will be stoked that you are living for him. But as I said already, God will help you in the marathon of the Christian life, through his word, prayer, his Spirit, and his people in church. That's why you want to start and keep reading the Bible, why you ought to start and keep talking to God in prayer, asking and thanking him for things day by day, and why it's so important to start and keep meeting with God's people in a Jesus-loving, Bible-believing church.

But through it all, remember that life with Jesus is the best life there is, and it will only get better into eternity.

Endnotes

1 Tacitus, *Annals*, XV:44.
2 Pliny the Younger, *Epistles*, 10:96.
3 Josephus, *Antiquities of the Jews*, 18:63.
4 Timothy Keller, *The Reason for God: Belief in an Age of Skepticism*, Hodder and Stoughton, London, 2008.
5 See John Stott, *The Cross of Christ*, IVP, Downers Grove, 1986, p. 159.

Feedback on this resource

If you enjoyed this Little Black Book, you might like to use the Facebook page as an easy way to let your friends know about it (as well as the other books in the series). And feel free to use the Facebook page to give me your feedback, comments and suggestions for future topics.

www.facebook.com/littleblackbooks

 matthiasmedia

Matthias Media is an evangelical publishing ministry that seeks to persuade all Christians of the truth of God's purposes in Jesus Christ as revealed in the Bible, and equip them with high-quality resources, so that by the work of the Holy Spirit they will:

- abandon their lives to the honour and service of Christ in daily holiness and decision-making
- pray constantly in Christ's name for the fruitfulness and growth of his gospel
- speak the Bible's life-changing word whenever and however they can—in the home, in the world and in the fellowship of his people.

To find out more about our large range of very useful resources, and to access samples and free downloads, visit our website:

www.matthiasmedia.com

How to buy our resources

1. Direct from us over the internet:
   – in the US: www.matthiasmedia.com
   – in Australia and the rest of the world: www.matthiasmedia.com.au

> Register at our website for our **free** regular email update to receive information about the latest new resources, **exclusive special offers**, and free articles to help you grow in your Christian life and ministry.

2. Direct from us by phone:
   – in the US: 1 866 407 4530
   – in Australia: 1300 051 220
   – international: +61 2 9233 4627

3. Through a range of outlets in various parts of the world. Visit **www.matthiasmedia.com/contact** for details about recommended retailers in your part of the world, including www.thegoodbook.co.uk in the United Kingdom.

4. Trade enquiries can be addressed to:
   – in the US and Canada: sales@matthiasmedia.com
   – in Australia and the rest of the world: sales@matthiasmedia.com.au

MORE

· Little Black Books ·

books that get to the point

Right Side Up

"I set out to write a book for new Christians, to explain what it means to be a Christian and what the lifelong adventure of following Jesus is like. But I soon realized that what Jesus wants to say to a new Christian is really the same thing he wants to keep saying to the seasoned saint: "Whoever loses his life for my sake will find it". My prayer is that this book will persuade you of the truth of those words, and help you live like you believe them. It's a book for the brand new Christian that should challenge every believer—whether you've been following Jesus for five minutes or fifty years."

—Author, Paul Grimmond

FOR MORE INFORMATION OR TO ORDER CONTACT:

Matthias Media
Ph: 1300 051 220
Int: +61 2 9233 4627
Email: sales@matthiasmedia.com.au
www.matthiasmedia.com.au

Matthias Media (USA)
Ph: 1 866 407 4530
Int: +1 330 953 1702
Email: sales@matthiasmedia.com
www.matthiasmedia.com

Hanging in There

Hanging in There is a book about God, you, the Bible, prayer, church, relationships, sex, feelings, doubts, love and, above all, hanging in there as a Christian. If you're a young Christian (teenager to early 20s), new to the Christian faith or a long-serving Christian who could use some encouragement, this book is for you.